HOW TO PRAY

Zanib Mian

C000193719

Published by Muslim Children's Books
Suite H, 31-33 College Road, Harrow, Middlesex HA1 1EJ

Muslim
Children's
Books

muslimchildrensbooks.co.uk

Published by Muslim Children's Books 2017
© Zanib Mian, 2017

Moral rights asserted.

ISBN 978-0-9955406-5-1

All rights reserved. No part of this publication may be reproduced, stored in a retrieval system, or transmitted in any form or by any means electronic,
mechanical, photocopying, recording or otherwise, without prior permission.

British Library Cataloguing in Publication Data. A catalogue record for this book is available from the British Library.

STEP   BY   STEP

HOW TO PRAY

" Imaginative and simple. A novel and easy approach
to learning wudu and prayer. "

- Dr Musharraf Hussain BSc, MA, PhD, Al-Azhari
OBE, DL

Zanib Mian

How to use this book

Look at this guy, to see what position your body should be in.

Read instructions with pointy arrows, with more details about your position. These are there because sometimes it's hard to see clearly what the stick guy is doing.

#1

Notice that all the steps are labelled, like this.

Say

Any words, in boxes like these, are said in the prayer. We have given these in Arabic text with transliteration, just in case you're still learning to read Arabic. Any other words on the page, which are not in a box like this, are not said in the prayer.

words words words
writing writing writing
text text text

Any other text on the page is an extra bit of information about that step of the prayer. You'll love these bits!

First

Make Wudu

To make wudu, or ablution, is to wash some parts of your body. Clean yourself before standing in front of Allah. You wouldn't want to talk to Allah when you're all mucky!

HERE'S HOW

WASH HANDS

Wash both of your hands, up to your wrists.

RINSE MOUTH

Rinse your mouth three times, by putting water into your mouth, swirling it around and then spitting it out.

Try not to splash!

#3

CLEAN NOSE

Sniff water into your nose. Not too much or too quickly – that hurts! Or you could wet your fingers and use them to clean the inside of your nose. Do this three times.

This is the only time you are allowed to put your fingers in your nose. Ever.

#4

WASH YOUR PRETTY LITTLE FACE

Wash your face three times. The water has to go all over the face, from one ear to the other and from where your hair begins to the chin. That means no dry patches, please!

#5

WASH ARMS

Now wash your arms, up to your elbows. First, the right arm, three times, then the left arm, three times.

a a a a a a h **that feels** *good.*

#6

MASAH

Masah means to wipe your head, with wet hands, from where your hair starts, all the way to the back. Do this once.

This is not washing your hair, so don't dip your head in the sink and don't use shampoo. If your fringe is dripping water, you have way overdone this.

9

#7 WIPE EARS

Next, use your wet pointing fingers to clean the inside part of your ear. Then use your thumbs to clean behind your ears. Just do this once too.

#8 WASH FEET

Wash your right foot, up to the ankles, three times. Then do the left foot. Get in between those toes to wash out any sock fluff and other dirt hiding there.

Don't do it with your shoes and socks on!

You did it! Ready to pray!

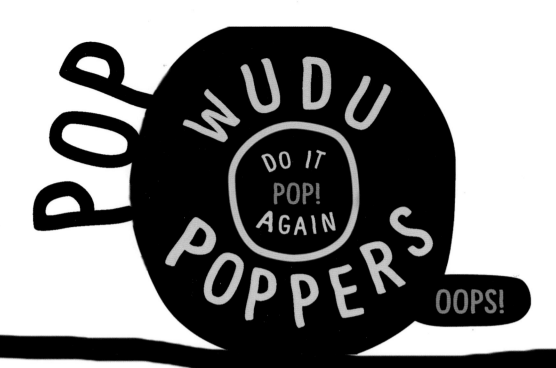

Some things can make your wudu pop, which means you have to do it again! Here they are:

And some other things that only adults need to worry about...

GOING TO THE TOILET

BLEEDING A LOT

SLEEPING!!!
UNLESS YOU SLEEP STANDING UP!

Z z Z z z z z

PASSING GAS

VOMITING

TIMING AND UNITS

There are 5 prayers that Allah has asked us to pray every day. They have certain timings, which change all the time, because they depend on the sun.

Below are the 5 daily prayers and the number of units that are done for each one. The fard units MUST be done. The sunnah units are optional. The sunnah units in pink are special and you should try your best to do them.

Prayer	Sunnah units before fard	Fard units	Sunnah units after fard
Fajr	2	2	0
Dhuhr	4	4	2
Asr	4	4	0
Maghrib	0	3	2
Isha	4	4	2 plus 3 witr

You can also pray extra units of prayer, if you feel like it. This is done 2 units at a time.

There are some times in the day at which you must not do this, These are: From Fajr until about 15 minutes after sunrise; when the sun is at its highest point in the sky; from Asr until the sun has set completely.

What are you wearing?

If you were about to meet a king, you would probably want to wear something nice and respectable. You wouldn't dream of going to meet him in your swimming costume! When you pray, you are standing before Allah, who is better than any king, so you should dress properly. When praying, we have to cover ourselves the way we would in front of others. For boys, this means covering yourself from your belly button to your knees. For girls, this means covering the whole body, except for the face, hands and feet.

QIBLA

Wherever you are in the world, you have to face towards the direction of the Ka'bah, in Makkah, to pray. This is called the Qibla. An adult will know which way this is, in your house. If you're praying away from home, you can be really smart and use a compass to find the direction of Makkah.

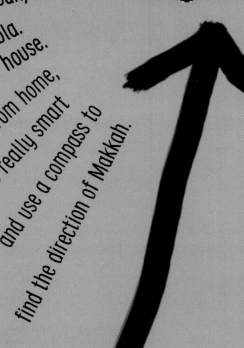

All Clean?

Before praying, you have to make sure that your **body,** your **clothes** and the **place** where you are praying are clean. That doesn't mean you have to get the vacuum cleaner out before every prayer, but there are some things that are not pure at all, so you have to make sure there are none of them around. These are: blood, vomit, urine, faeces (poo), and other impure things.

15

Ready?

Steady?

Pray!

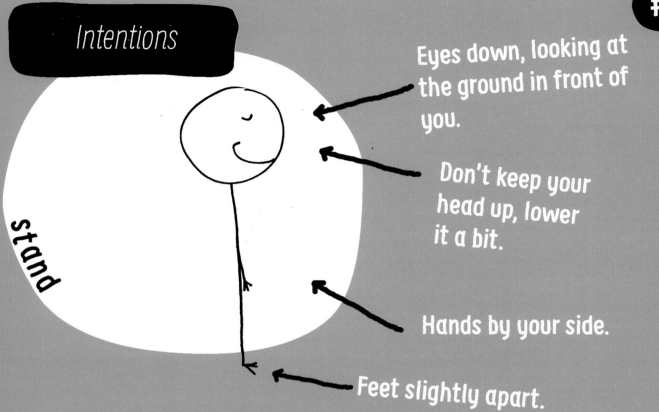

Intentions

stand

Eyes down, looking at the ground in front of you.

Don't keep your head up, lower it a bit.

Hands by your side.

Feet slightly apart.

Before you start praying, think about what you are about to do. This is your intention. You don't have to say it out loud, you can just think it in your head. You should think about these things:

> How many units of salah you are going to do.
> Which salah you are praying.
> That you are doing it for Allah.
> That you are facing the Qibla.

WHY?

This is all so that you can get focused, because you are about to talk to Allah! You put your head down because it shows respect.

Allahu Akbar

This means Allah is the Greatest.

Raise hands

Raise your hands to the level of your shoulders or ears, with the palms facing forwards.

Look at the ground, one or two steps in front of you.

why?

You're beginning the prayer! You take away all other thoughts and images from your mind. So you have to stop thinking about your exciting new game, or where you're going tomorrow! When you raise your hands like this, you can imagine that you're throwing all those other thoughts behind you, where they can wait till after you've finished!

stand

Say

subhanakal-lahumma wabihamdika

سُبْحَانَكَ اللَّهُمَّ وَ بِحَمْدِكَ

watabarakas-muka wata'aala jadduka wa la ilaha ghayruk.

وَ تَبَارَكَ اسْمُكَ وَ تَعَالَى

جَدُّكَ وَ لَا إِلَهَ غَيْرُكَ

This dua is Sunnah. It's important, but you can still do your salah without it.

Put your right hand over your left hand over your chest. Some people place their hands over their belly. Ask your adult where you should put yours.

This means:

Glory be to you, O Allah, and all praises are due unto You,

and blessed is Your name and high is Your majesty

and none is worthy of worship but You

#4

stand

Stay in the same position as #3 and keep looking at the floor. No peeking here or there!

Guess what?

You're speaking to Allah! Telling him that you would never worship anyone but Him. You ask for His help and ask Him to guide you.

say

Aoodhu billahi minash-shaytanir-rajeem

أَعُوذُ بِاللهِ مِنَ الشَّيْطَانِ الرَّجِيمِ

Bismillaahir Rahmaanir Raheem

بِسْمِ اللَّهِ الرَّحْمَنِ الرَّحِيمِ

Alhamdu lillaahi Rabbil 'aalameen

الْحَمْدُ لِلَّهِ رَبِّ الْعَالَمِينَ

Ar-Rahmaanir-Raheem

الرَّحْمَنِ الرَّحِيمِ

Maaliki Yawmid-Deen

مَالِكِ يَوْمِ الدِّينِ

Iyyaaka na'budu wa Iyyaaka nasta'een

إِيَّاكَ نَعْبُدُ وَإِيَّاكَ نَسْتَعِينُ

Ihdinas-Siraatal-Mustaqeem

اهْدِنَا الصِّرَاطَ الْمُسْتَقِيمَ

Siraatal-lazeena an'amta 'alaihim

صِرَاطَ الَّذِينَ أَنْعَمْتَ عَلَيْهِمْ

Ghayril-maghdoobi 'alaihim wa lad-daaalleen. Aameen.

غَيْرِ الْمَغْضُوبِ عَلَيْهِمْ وَلَا الضَّالِّينَ آمِين

#5

stand

Any Surah/Chapter from the Quran.

For *example Surah Ikhlas*

Bismillaahir Rahmaanir Raheem

بِسْمِ اللَّهِ الرَّحْمَنِ الرَّحِيمِ

Qul huwal laahu ahad

قُلْ هُوَ اللَّهُ أَحَدٌ

Allah hus-samad

اللَّهُ الصَّمَدُ

Lam yalid wa lam yoolad

لَمْ يَلِدْ وَلَمْ يُولَدْ

Wa lam yakul-lahu kufuwan ahad

وَلَمْ يَكُنْ لَهُ كُفُوًا أَحَدٌ

This Surah is awesome! You're saying that Allah is the one and only. The one who will always be. He doesn't have children and He doesn't have parents. Nothing can compare to Him and there is nothing like Him.

#6

Say **Allahu Akbar**
الله أَكْبَرْ

Some people *raise hands* while saying *Allahu Akbar*

Bow

And go into a bowing position like this.

Try to make a 90 degree angle with your body and keep your eyes on the floor.

Then say

Subhanna Rabbiyal Adheem
سُبْحَانَ رَبِّيَ الْعَظِيمْ

Say it 3 times

why?

You're bowing to Allah, because He is glorious and He is supreme. You're feeling humble in front of Him. You're saying 'Glory be to my Lord, the greatest.' Yes, YOUR Lord! You're feeling very close to Him.

While coming back up to the standing position

Say

Sami'Allah huliman hamidah

سَمِعَ اللهُ لِمَنْ حَمِدَه

This means that Allah listens to those who praise Him.

So you know that you're not doing this for no reason.
Allah is listening!

stand

Say

Rabbana Walakal Hamd

رَبَّنَا وَ لَكَ الْحَمْد

This means:

Our Lord, all praise is for You!

And next you're going to do the most amazing part of the prayer...

24

SUJOOD

Say

Allahu Akbar
الله أَكْبَرْ

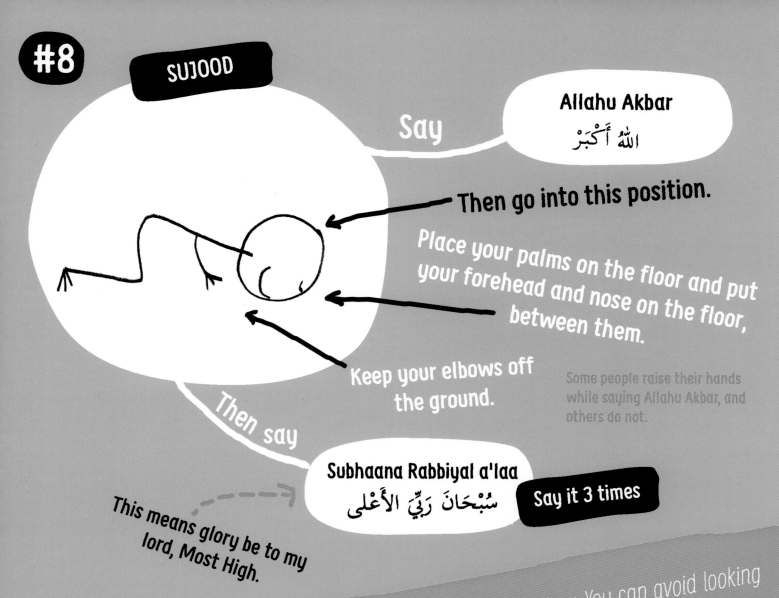

Then go into this position.

Place your palms on the floor and put your forehead and nose on the floor, between them.

Keep your elbows off the ground.

Some people raise their hands while saying Allahu Akbar, and others do not.

Then say

Subhaana Rabbiyal a'laa
سُبْحَانَ رَبِّيَ الأَعْلى

Say it 3 times

This means glory be to my lord, Most High.

Some people do this bit like they've suddenly fallen onto the floor. You can avoid looking like that has happened to you by taking your time to get into this position. Do it as smoothly and as elegantly as possible. Remember, you are not diving into a pool.

Say **Allahu Akbar**
الله أَكْبَرْ

As you sit up.

Sit

Sit with your hands on your thighs, near your knees.

PAUSE

There's a special way to put your feet, if you can manage. The left foot is tucked under you and the toes of the right foot are the only part of the foot touching the floor and facing the Qibla. An adult can show you this.

If you want, while you pause you can say **Rabbighfirlee**
رَبِّ اغْفِرْلِي

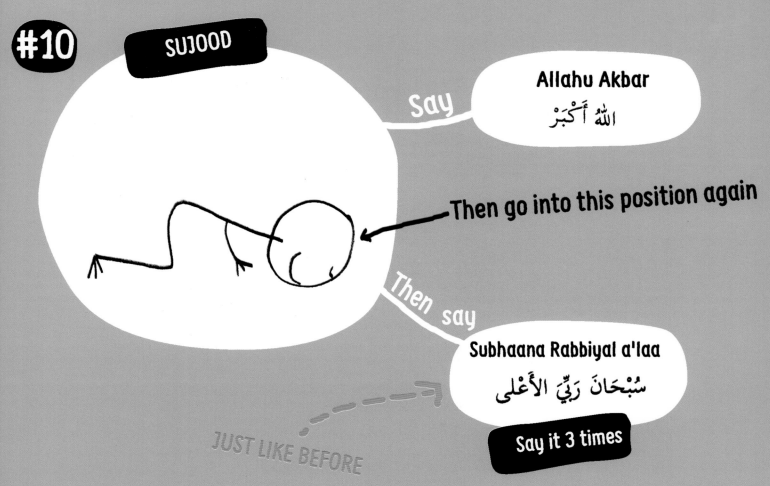

#11

Say

Aoodhu billahi minash-shaytanir-rajeem

أَعُوذُ بِاللهِ مِنَ الشَّيْطَانِ الرَّجِيمِ

Bismillaahir Rahmaanir Raheem

بِسْمِ اللَّهِ الرَّحْمَنِ الرَّحِيمِ

Alhamdu lillaahi Rabbil 'aalameen

الْحَمْدُ لِلَّهِ رَبِّ الْعَالَمِينَ

Ar-Rahmaanir-Raheem

الرَّحْمَنِ الرَّحِيمِ

Maaliki Yawmid-Deen

مَالِكِ يَوْمِ الدِّينِ

Iyyaaka na'budu wa Iyyaaka nasta'een

إِيَّاكَ نَعْبُدُ وَإِيَّاك نَسْتَعِينُ

Ihdinas-Siraatal-Mustaqeem

اهْدِنَا الصِّرَاطَ الْمُسْتَقِيمَ

Siraatal-lazeena an'amta 'alaihim

صِرَاطَ الَّذِينَ أَنْعَمْتَ عَلَيْهِمْ

Ghayril-maghdoobi 'alaihim wa
lad-daaalleen. Aameen.

غَيْرِ الْمَغْضُوبِ عَلَيْهِمْ وَلا الضَّالِّينَ آمِين

You said this before,
in #4. This Surah is called
Fatiha.

28

#12

Any Surah/Chapter from the Quran.

Here's one

This is Surah Naas. It protects us from the big, bad meanies of the world!

Bismillaahir Rahmaanir Raheem

بِسْمِ اللَّهِ الرَّحْمَنِ الرَّحِيمِ

Qul A'uothoo BiRabbinaas

قُلْ أَعُوذُ بِرَبِّ النَّاسِ

Malikinnaas

مَلِكِ النَّاسِ

ilaahinnaas

إِلَهِ النَّاسِ

Min Sharril Waswaasil Khanaas

مِنْ شَرِّ الْوَسْوَاسِ الْخَنَّاسِ

Allahthee Yuwaswisu Fee sudoorinnaas

الَّذِي يُوَسْوِسُ فِي صُدُورِ النَّاسِ

Minal Jinnati Wannaas

مِنَ الْجِنَّةِ وَالنَّاسِ

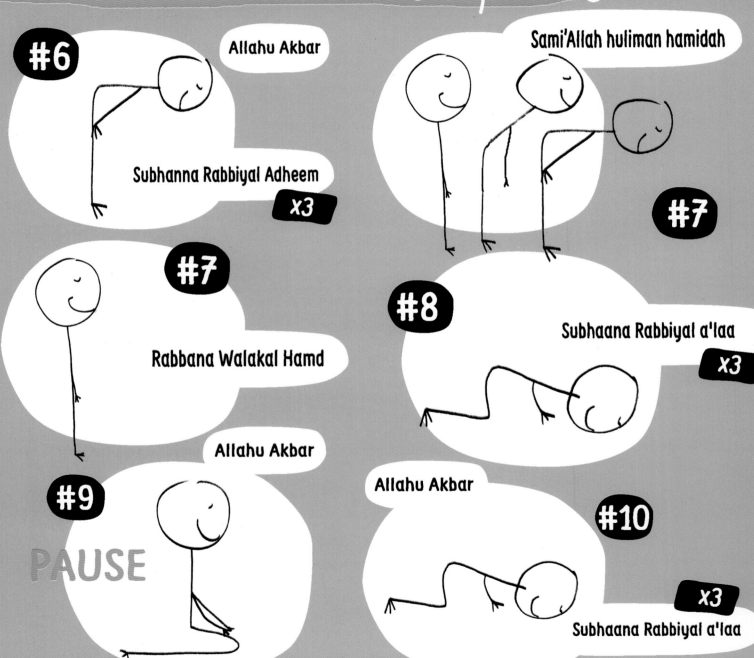

#13

Sit

Say

Allahu Akbar

As you sit up again

Attahiyaatu lillahi wassalawatu Watayyabaatu

التَّحِيَّاتُ لِلَّهِ وَالصَّلَوَاتُ وَالطَّيِّبَات

Assalaamu 'alayka ayyuhannabiyu

السَّلَامُ عَلَيْكَ أَيُّهَا النَّبِيُّ

Warahmatullahi wabarakaatuhu

وَرَحْمَةُ اللهِ وَبَرَكاتُه

Assalaamu 'alayna wa'alaa ibaadillah-hissaaliheen

السَّلَامُ عَلَيْنا وَ عَلى عِبادِ اللهِ الصَّالِحِين

#14

Say

Sit

Ash-hadu al-aa ilaaha ill-Allaah

أَشْهَدُ أَنْ لاَ إِلَهَ إِلاَّ الله

wa ash-hadu anna Muhammadan 'abduhu wa rasooluhu

وَأَشْهَدُ أَنَّ مُحَمَّداً عَبْدُهُ وَرَسُوله

Keep your hands in your lap and lift the pointing finger of your right hand while saying this.

This is so wonderful! You're saying that you know for sure that there is no God except Allah and that Muhammad (sallallahu alayhi Wasallam) is his servant and messenger.

2 units of prayer are almost done! If you are praying 2 units, carry on to step #15.

If you are doing 3 units of prayer, you need to stand one more time, skip forward to page 37 to see how.

If you are doing 4 units of prayer, you need to stand two more times, skip forward to page 45 to see how.

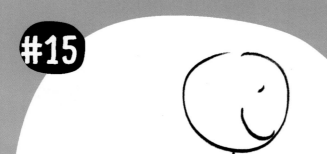

#15

Say

Keep your hands in your lap and put the pointing finger down again.

Allaahumma salli 'ala Muhammad

اللَّهُمَّ صَلِّ عَلَى مُحَمَّد

wa 'ala aali Muhammad

وَ عَلى آلِ مُحَمَّد

kama salayta 'ala Ibraaheem

كَما صَلَّيْتَ عَلى إِبْراهِيم

wa 'ala aali Ibraaheem,
innaka hameedun majeed

وَعَلى آلِ إِبْراهِيم إِنَّكَ حَمِيدٌ مَجِيد

Wa baarik 'ala Muhammad,
wa 'ala aali Muhammad

وَبَارِكْ عَلى مُحَمَّدٍ وَعَلى آلِ مُحَمَّد

kama baarakta 'ala Ibraaheem

كَما بَارَكْتَ عَلى إِبْراهِيم

wa 'ala aali Ibraaheem

وَعَلى آلِ إِبْراهِيم

innak hameedun majeed

إِنَّكَ حَمِيدٌ مَجِيد

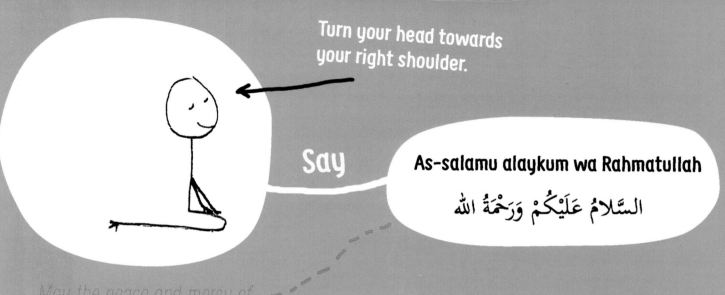

Turn your head towards your right shoulder.

Say

As-salamu alaykum wa Rahmatullah

السَّلامُ عَلَيْكُمْ وَرَحْمَةُ الله

May the peace and mercy of Allah be with you.

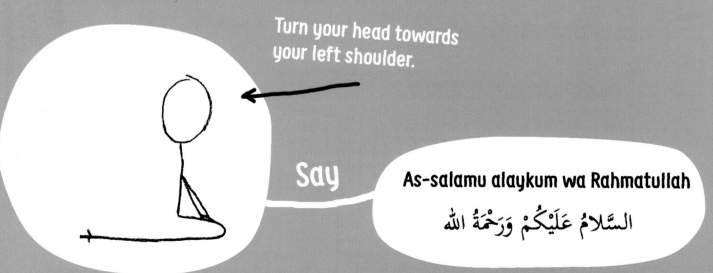

Turn your head towards your left shoulder.

Say

As-salamu alaykum wa Rahmatullah

السَّلامُ عَلَيْكُمْ وَرَحْمَةُ الله

YOUR 2 UNIT PRAYER IS COMPLETE
AMAZING!

NOW MAKE
DUA

Ask Allah for anything!!!

LOOK FORWARD TO THE NEXT ONE

For a 3 unit prayer

(carrying on from #14)

#4

stand

Say

Carry on enjoying your prayer and staying focused on only Allah

Aoodhu billahi minash-shaytanir-rajeem

أَعُوذُ بِاللهِ مِنَ الشَّيْطَانِ الرَّجِيمِ

Bismillaahir Rahmaanir Raheem

بِسْمِ اللَّهِ الرَّحْمَنِ الرَّحِيمِ

Alhamdu lillaahi Rabbil 'aalameen

الْحَمْدُ لِلَّهِ رَبِّ الْعَالَمِينَ

Ar-Rahmaanir-Raheem

الرَّحْمَنِ الرَّحِيمِ

Maaliki Yawmid-Deen

مَالِكِ يَوْمِ الدِّينِ

Iyyaaka na'budu wa Iyyaaka nasta'een

إِيَّاكَ نَعْبُدُ وَإِيَّاكَ نَسْتَعِينُ

Ihdinas-Siraatal-Mustaqeem

اهْدِنَا الصِّرَاطَ الْمُسْتَقِيمَ

Siraatal-lazeena an'amta 'alaihim

صِرَاطَ الَّذِينَ أَنْعَمْتَ عَلَيْهِمْ

Ghayril-maghdoobi 'alaihim wa lad-daaalleen. Aameen.

غَيْرِ الْمَغْضُوبِ عَلَيْهِمْ وَلَا الضَّالِّينَ آمِين

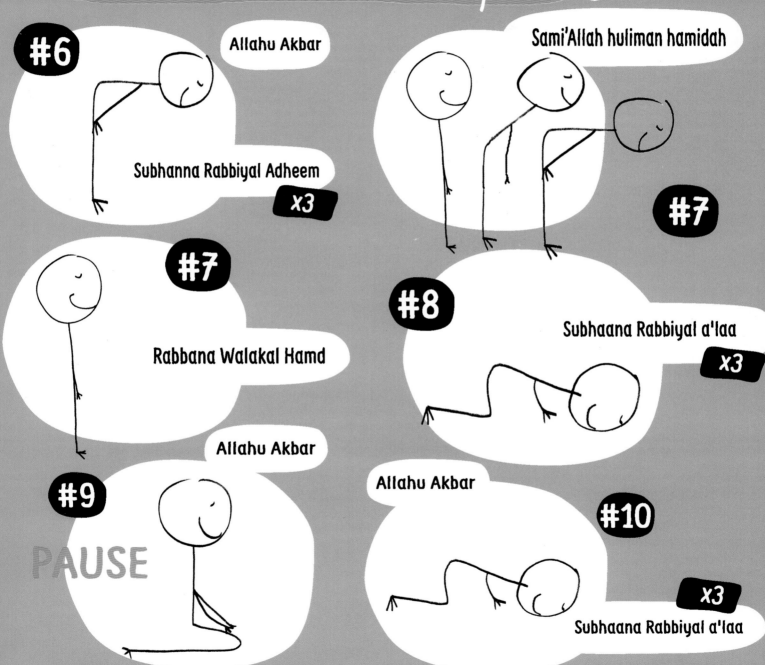

#13

Sit

Say

Allahu Akbar

As you sit up again

Attahiyaatu lillahi wassalawatu Watayyabaatu

التَّحِيَّاتُ لِلهِ والصَّلَوَاتُ والطَّيِّبَات

Assalaamu 'alayka ayyuhannabiyu

السَّلامُ عَلَيْكَ أَيُّها النَّبِيُّ

Warahmatullahi wabarakaatuhu

وَرَحْمَةُ اللهِ وَبَرَكاتُه

Assalaamu 'alayna wa'alaa ibaadillah-hissaaliheen

السَّلامُ عَلَيْنا وَ عَلى عِبادِ اللهِ الصَّالِحِين

#14

Sit

Say

Ash-hadu al-aa ilaaha ill-Allaah

أَشْهَدُ أَنْ لاَ إِلَهَ إِلاَّ الله

wa ash-hadu anna Muhammadan 'abduhu wa rasooluhu

وَأَشْهَدُ أَنَّ مُحَمَّداً عَبْدُهُ وَرَسُوله

Keep your hands in your lap and lift the pointing finger of your right hand while saying this.

#15

Keep your hands in your lap and put the pointing finger down again.

Say

Allaahumma salli 'ala Muhammad

اللَّهُمَّ صَلِّ عَلَى مُحَمَّد

wa 'ala aali Muhammad

وَ عَلَى آلِ مُحَمَّد

kama salayta 'ala Ibraaheem

كَما صَلَّيْتَ عَلَى إِبْراهيم

wa 'ala aali Ibraaheem,
innaka hameedun majeed

وَعَلى آلِ إِبْراهيم إِنَّكَ حَميدٌ مَجيد

Wa baarik 'ala Muhammad,
wa 'ala aali Muhammad

وَبَارِكْ عَلَى مُحَمَّدٍ وَعَلَى آلِ مُحَمَّد

kama baarakta 'ala Ibraaheem

كَما بَارَكْتَ عَلَى إِبْراهيم

wa 'ala aali Ibraaheem

وَعَلى آلِ إِبْراهيم

innak hameedun majeed

إِنَّكَ حَميدٌ مَجيد

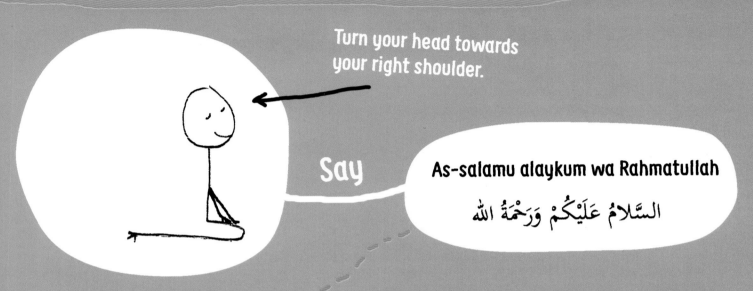

Turn your head towards your right shoulder.

Say

As-salamu alaykum wa Rahmatullah

السَّلَامُ عَلَيْكُمْ وَرَحْمَةُ الله

May the peace and mercy of Allah be with you.

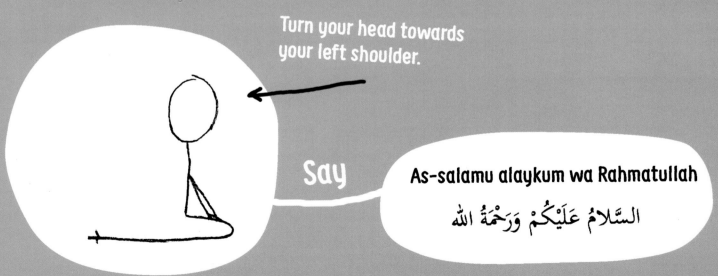

Turn your head towards your left shoulder.

Say

As-salamu alaykum wa Rahmatullah

السَّلَامُ عَلَيْكُمْ وَرَحْمَةُ الله

YOUR 3 UNIT PRAYER IS COMPLETE
AMAZING!

NOW MAKE

DUA

Ask Allah for anything!!!

LOOK FORWARD TO THE NEXT ONE

For a 4 unit prayer

(carrying on from #14)

#4

stand

say

Carry on enjoying your prayer and staying focused on only Allah

Aoodhu billahi minash-shaytanir-rajeem

أَعُوذُ بِاللهِ مِنَ الشَّيْطَانِ الرَّجِيمِ

Bismillaahir Rahmaanir Raheem

بِسْمِ اللَّهِ الرَّحْمَنِ الرَّحِيمِ

Alhamdu lillaahi Rabbil 'aalameen

الْحَمْدُ لِلَّهِ رَبِّ الْعَالَمِينَ

Ar-Rahmaanir-Raheem

الرَّحْمَنِ الرَّحِيمِ

Maaliki Yawmid-Deen

مَالِكِ يَوْمِ الدِّينِ

Iyyaaka na'budu wa Iyyaaka nasta'een

إِيَّاكَ نَعْبُدُ وَإِيَّاكَ نَسْتَعِينُ

Ihdinas-Siraatal-Mustaqeem

اهْدِنَا الصِّرَاطَ الْمُسْتَقِيمَ

Siraatal-lazeena an'amta 'alaihim

صِرَاطَ الَّذِينَ أَنْعَمْتَ عَلَيْهِمْ

Ghayril-maghdoobi 'alaihim wa lad-daaalleen. Aameen.

غَيْرِ الْمَغْضُوبِ عَلَيْهِمْ وَلا الضَّالِّينَ آمِين

46

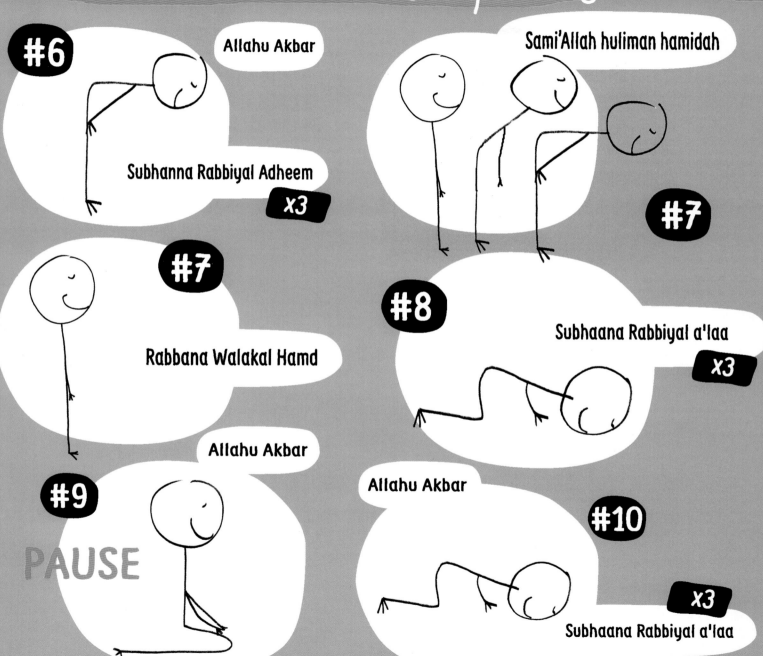

#4

say

stand

Carry on enjoying your prayer and staying focused on only Allah

Aoodhu billahi minash-shaytanir-rajeem

أَعُوذُ بِاللهِ مِنَ الشَّيْطَانِ الرَّجِيمِ

Bismillaahir Rahmaanir Raheem

بِسْمِ اللَّهِ الرَّحْمَنِ الرَّحِيمِ

Alhamdu lillaahi Rabbil 'aalameen

الْحَمْدُ لِلَّهِ رَبِّ الْعَالَمِينَ

Ar-Rahmaanir-Raheem

الرَّحْمَنِ الرَّحِيمِ

Maaliki Yawmid-Deen

مَالِكِ يَوْمِ الدِّينِ

Iyyaaka na'budu wa Iyyaaka nasta'een

إِيَّاكَ نَعْبُدُ وَإِيَّاك نَسْتَعِينُ

Ihdinas-Siraatal-Mustaqeem

اهْدِنَا الصِّرَاطَ الْمُسْتَقِيمَ

Siraatal-lazeena an'amta 'alaihim

صِرَاطَ الَّذِينَ أَنْعَمْتَ عَلَيْهِمْ

Ghayril-maghdoobi 'alaihim wa lad-daaalleen. Aameen.

غَيْرِ الْمَغْضُوبِ عَلَيْهِمْ وَلا الضَّالِّينَ آمِين

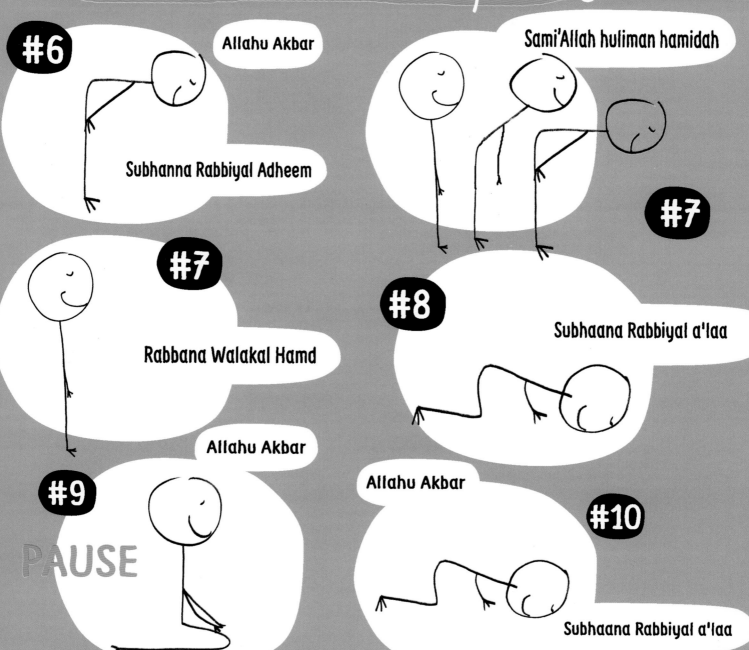

Then do this step again

Say

Allahu Akbar

As you sit up again

Sit

Attahiyaatu lillahi wassalawatu Watayyabaatu

التَّحِيَّاتُ لِلَّهِ والصَّلَواتُ والطَّيِّبَات

Assalaamu 'alayka ayyuhannabiyu

السَّلَامُ عَلَيْكَ أَيُّها النَّبِيُّ

Warahmatullahi wabarakaatuhu

وَرَحْمَةُ اللهِ وَبَرَكاتُه

Assalaamu 'alayna wa'alaa ibaadillah-hissaaliheen

السَّلَامُ عَلَيْنا وَعَلى عِبادِ اللهِ الصَّالِحِين

...and this step again

#14

Say

Ash-hadu al-aa ilaaha ill-Allaah

أَشْهَدُ أَنْ لاَ إِلَهَ إِلاَّ الله

wa ash-hadu anna Muhammadan 'abduhu wa rasooluhu

وَأَشْهَدُ أَنَّ مُحَمَّداً عَبْدُهُ وَرَسُوله

Sit

Keep your hands in your lap and lift the pointing finger of your right hand while saying this.

#15

Keep your hands in your lap and put the pointing finger down again.

Say

Allaahumma salli 'ala Muhammad

اللَّهُمَّ صَلِّ عَلى مُحَمَّد

wa 'ala aali Muhammad

وَ عَلى آلِ مُحَمَّد

kama salayta 'ala Ibraaheem

كَما صَلَّيْتَ عَلى إِبْراهيم

wa 'ala aali Ibraaheem,
innaka hameedun majeed

وَعَلى آلِ إِبْراهيم إِنَّكَ حَميدٌ مَجيد

Wa baarik 'ala Muhammad,
wa 'ala aali Muhammad

وَبارِك عَلى مُحَمَّدٍ وَعَلى آلِ مُحَمَّد

kama baarakta 'ala Ibraaheem

كَما بَارَكْتَ عَلى إِبْراهِيم

wa 'ala aali Ibraaheem

وَعَلى آلِ إِبْراهيم

innak hameedun majeed

إِنَّكَ حَميدٌ مَجيد

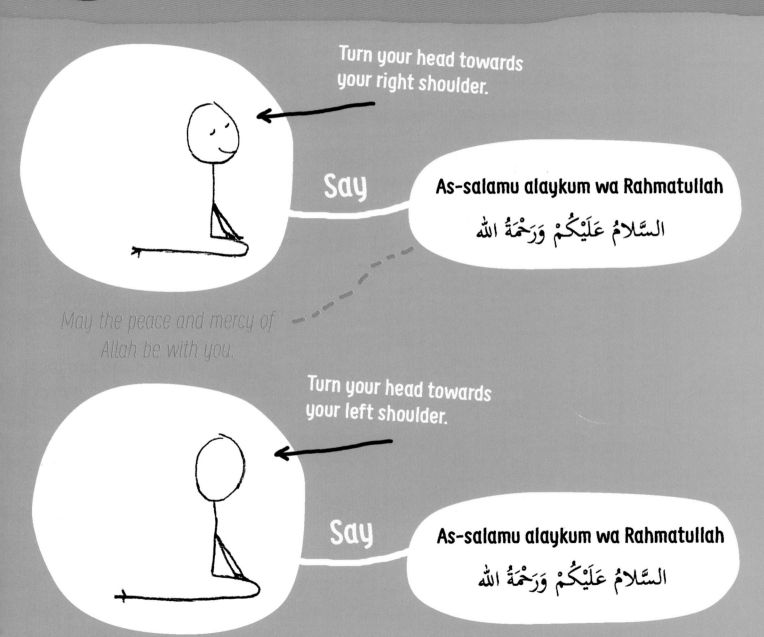

Turn your head towards your right shoulder.

Say

As-salamu alaykum wa Rahmatullah

السَّلَامُ عَلَيْكُمْ وَرَحْمَةُ الله

May the peace and mercy of Allah be with you.

Turn your head towards your left shoulder.

Say

As-salamu alaykum wa Rahmatullah

السَّلَامُ عَلَيْكُمْ وَرَحْمَةُ الله

YOUR 4 UNIT PRAYER IS COMPLETE

AMAZING!

NOW MAKE

DUA

Ask Allah for anything!!!

LOOK FORWARD TO THE NEXT ONE

Write about how prayer makes you feel

More fantastic titles by MuslimChildren's Books Ltd

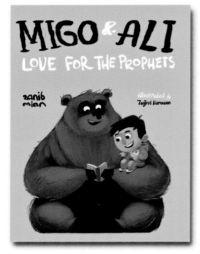

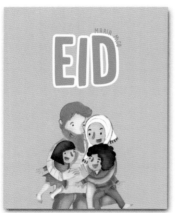

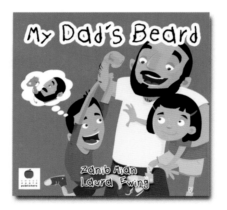

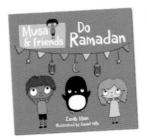

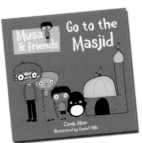

www.muslimchildrensbooks.co.uk